# BTEC
# SPORT
## ASSESSMENT GUIDE

## Unit 3 THE MIND AND SPORTS PERFORMANCE

KATHERINE HOWARD

Edited by
Jennifer Stafford-Brown & Simon Rea

**HODDER**
EDUCATION
AN HACHETTE UK COMPANY

The sample learner answers provided in this assessment guide are intended to give guidance on how a learner might approach generating evidence for each assessment criterion. Answers do not necessarily include all of the evidence required to meet each assessment criterion. Assessor comments intend to highlight how sample answers might be improved to help learners meet the requirements of the grading criterion but are provided as a guide only. Sample answers and assessor guidance have not been verified by Edexcel and any information provided in this guide should not replace your own internal verification process.

Any work submitted as evidence for assessment for this unit must be the learner's own. Submitting as evidence, in whole or in part, any material taken from this guide will be regarded as plagiarism. Hodder Education accepts no responsibility for learners plagiarising work from this guide that does or does not meet the assessment criteria.

The sample assignment briefs are provided as a guide to how you might assess the evidence required for all or part of the internal assessment of this Unit. They have not been verified or endorsed by Edexcel and should be internally verified through your own Lead Internal Verifier as with any other assignment briefs, and/or checked through the BTEC assignment checking service.

Every effort has been made to trace the copyright holders of material reproduced here. The authors and publishers would like to thank the following for permission to reproduce copyright illustrations.

Figure 1.1 © Rob Bouwman – Fotolia; Figures 1.3 and 1.4 © Toutenphoton – Fotolia; Figure 2.1 © YASUYOSHI CHIBA/AFP/GettyImages; Figure 2.2 © Jari Hindström – Fotolia; Figure 2.3 © Bryn Lennon/Getty Images; Figure 2.4 © GIS – Fotolia; Figure 3.1 © Cultura/Peter Muller/Getty Images.

Orders: please contact Bookpoint Ltd, 130 Milton Park, Abingdon, Oxon OX14 4SB. Telephone: (44) 01235 827720. Fax: (44) 01235 400454. Lines are open from 9.00–5.00, Monday to Saturday, with a 24 hour message answering service. You can also order through our website www.hoddereducation.co.uk

If you have any comments to make about this, or any of our other titles, please send them to educationenquiries@hodder.co.uk

*British Library Cataloguing in Publication Data*

A catalogue record for this title is available from the British Library

ISBN: 978 1 444 1 86659

Published 2013

Impression number   10 9 8 7 6 5 4 3 2 1

Year         2016 2015 2014 2013

Copyright © 2013 Katherine Howard, Jennifer Stafford-Brown and Simon Rea

Cover photo © Sergey Yarochkin – Fotolia

Typeset by Integra Software Services Pvt. Ltd., Pondicherry, India

Printed in Dubai for Hodder Education, an Hachette UK Company, 338 Euston Road, London NW1 3BH

# Contents

## For attention of the learner

You are not allowed to copy any information from this book and use it as your own evidence. That would count as plagiarism, which is taken very seriously and may result in disqualification. If you are in any doubt at all please speak to your teacher.

# Command words

You will find the following command words in the assessment criteria for each unit.

| Analyse | Identify the factors that apply and state how these are related. Explain the importance of each one. |
|---|---|
| Assess | Give careful consideration to all the factors or events that apply and identify which are the most important or relevant. |
| Describe | Give a clear description that includes all the relevant features – think of it as 'painting a picture with words'. |
| Discuss | Consider different aspects of a topic and how they interrelate, and the extent to which they are important. |
| Evaluate | Bring together all the information and review it to form a conclusion. Give evidence for each of your views or statements. |
| Explain | Provide details and give reasons and/or evidence to support the arguments being made. Start by introducing the topic then give the 'how' or 'why'. |
| Summarise | Demonstrate an understanding of the key facts, and if possible illustrate with relevant examples. |

# Introduction

Unit 3, The Mind and Sports Performance, is an internally assessed, optional, specialist unit with three learning aims:

- Learning aim A: Investigate personality and its effect on sports performance
- Learning aim B: Explore the influence that motivation and self-confidence have on sports performance
- Learning aim C: Know about arousal and anxiety, and the effects they have on sports performance.

The unit focuses on what influences the mind in sport and how this can affect performance. Learning aim A covers personality and how this can influence the sports we choose and impact our performance in those sports. Learning aim B looks at the impact of motivation and self-confidence on performance and techniques that can be used to influence them. Finally, in learning aim C, we look at the role of arousal and anxiety in sport.

Each learning aim is divided in to two sections. The first section focuses on the content of the learning aim and each of the topics are covered. At the end of each section there are some knowledge recap questions to test your understanding of the subject. The answers for the knowledge recap questions can be found at the end of the book.

The second section of each learning aim provides support with assessment by using evidence generated by a student, for each grading criterion, with feedback from an assessor. The assessor has highlighted where the evidence is sufficient to satisfy the grading criterion and provided developmental feedback when additional work is required.

At the end of the book are examples of assignment briefs for this unit. There is a sample assignment for each learning aim, and the tasks allow you to generate the evidence needed to meet all the assessment criteria in the unit.

# Learning aim A
## Investigate personality and its effect on sports performance

### Assessment criteria

**2A.P1** Using relevant examples, describe personality, including methods of measurement and three different views.

**2A.M1** Explain three different views of personality, and how personality can affect sports performance.

**2A.D1** Analyse three different views of personality, and how personality can affect sports performance.

## Topic A.1 Definition of personality

Figure 1.1 A person's personality can affect performance

Personality is the sum of the characteristics that make a person unique. For a sports person to be successful, it is important that the coach knows what personality type he or she is so that the correct psychological training methods can be applied to ensure the performer's success. Performers need to be aware how personality characteristics can affect their performances, for example, mood, anxiety (negative emotional feelings, caused by a fear of a new situation or the fear of failing), arousal level (an increased state of readiness, having motivated behaviour) so that they can deal with them and minimise their impact on performance.

Personality is stable and unique to every person. Personality affects how we respond to different situations. It involves our character, intellect, physique and temperament. Personality can be the link to improving sports performance.

# Topic A.2 Structure of personality

## Role-related behaviours

Studied ☐

In different situations a person's behaviour will change, depending on the role to be taken on and how the person perceives the environment or situation at any moment in time. Role-related behaviour is the most changeable aspect of personality. Role-related behaviour could explain a person behaving irrationally due to the way he or she has interpreted a situation.

In sport a person may take on the role of a captain and his or her behaviour will change to adapt to that situation. The captain will need to show leadership and confidence. The same person may play as a reserve for another team and show submission, following instructions without question.

## Typical responses

Studied ☐

Typical responses are the ways we will usually respond to a situation. For example, a good team captain might always stay positive, even when the team are losing so that he or she can help to motivate team members and ensure that the team goes on to win successfully.

A typical response is learned from repeating the same response over and over again. A person who has failed at a skill may believe he or she can never do it and the typical response would be a negative one towards performing or even trying the skill. For example, if a gymnast attempts to perform a backward roll and fails, tries again and fails and is unsuccessful at every attempt after that, he or she will respond with the same response: 'I can't do it'.

## Psychological core

Studied ☐

The psychological core is made up of a person's different attitudes, values, interests and beliefs. This is the real you.

The psychological core contains the idea of the true self and is never revealed. Personality tests cannot penetrate the psychological core and so a true prediction of personality cannot really ever be made. Typical responses to situations can be seen as a measure of your psychological core and they give a good indication of a person's behaviours.

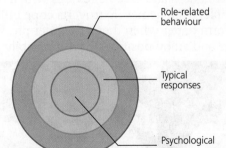

Figure 1.2 The psychological core

# Topic A.3 Personality types

Personalities have been described as introverts and extroverts. People tend not to be one or the other but somewhere in between both.

## Introverts

Studied

Introverts tend to be inward looking and shy; they are comfortable in their own company. These types of people may prefer individual sports activities with little movement, which require refined skills, and sports with repetitive actions, for example, long distance swimming, shooting or archery. Introverts do not need to be with other people to get them ready, aroused for their competition. In fact introverts try to avoid situations of over-arousal and choose activities which need accuracy rather than force.

Figure 1.3 Some people prefer solitary sports

## Extroverts

Studied

Extroverts tend to be outgoing and comfortable in other people's company. These types of people may prefer team sports and activities which use the whole body. These types of people tend to be very confident and enjoy activities with a degree of uncertainty, for example, team games. Extroverts cope much better with arousal and perform better when they are under pressure. They like a challenge and enjoy positions of responsibility.

Figure 1.4 Some people enjoy team sports

## Type A and type B

Studied

Personalities have been split into two types. Type A personalities have a competitive drive and are prone to anger and hostility. These people can be impatient, intolerant and have high levels of stress.

Type B personalities are generally laid back and have a calm disposition. These people can be more relaxed, have a tolerant approach and have lower levels of stress and competition. It is thought that type A personalities are more likely to succeed in competitive sports situations than type B, but there is little evidence to confirm whether personality will make a person a better sports person.

## Effects of personality on sports performance

Studied

### Team versus individual sports

There is little evidence to suggest that there is an ideal sports personality type, but there are some differences between those who play team sports and those who prefer individual sports. Athletes who choose team sports tend to be more extrovert and those who prefer individual sports are often more introverted. There will be exceptions to this and it is difficult to draw conclusions until we have looked at the sports being played.

### Athletes and non-athletes

Research might suggest that athletes have higher levels of competitiveness and lower levels of depression and fatigue. To make any definitive statement more research needs to be carried out and on a larger range of athletes and sports. However, from what we know about personality types, successful sports people are more likely to be type A and more extroverted than introverted. Athletes need a drive to push them on to win, this is shown in type A personalities and the desire to win and respond positively to arousal would mean that extroverts would thrive on the pressure of competition.

## Knowledge recap

1. What is personality?

2. Why is it important for a coach to know an athlete's personality type?

3. What is meant by 'typical responses'?

4. What makes up the 'psychological core'?

5. What are introvert personality types?

6. What are extrovert personality types?

# Topic A.4 Methods of measuring personality

## Questionnaires

Studied

Personality types or characteristics can be measured by using a questionnaire.

### EPI (Eysenck's Personality Inventory)

Eysenck's personality inventory or EPI can be completed by the sports coach or the athlete and results are recorded and assessed.

Eysenck recognised four personality types:

- Unstable (neurotic) and extroverted
- Stable and extroverted
- Stable and introverted
- Unstable (neurotic) and introverted

Eysenck's questionnaire will show where on the model personality falls. A stable personality implies that the person is even-tempered and reliable. Unstable personalities may be changeable and impulsive. Extroverts will be outgoing and talkative whereas introverts may be quiet and reserved. By identifying which personality characteristics a person has, the coach can ensure the right psychological techniques are used to get the best out of the person being coached.

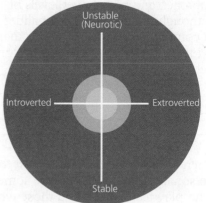

Figure 1.5 Eysenck's two-dimensional personality model

### POMS (Profile of Mood States)

Profile of Mood States or POMS is a psychological rating scale used to measure and identify different mood states.

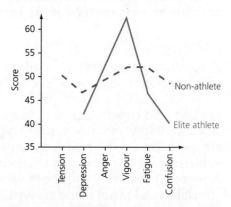

Figure 1.6 POMS results for non-athletes and elite athletes

## Observation

Studied

Personality can be measured by observing the athlete's traits or characteristics and behaviours. By observing the athlete, a coach can assess which personality traits are most commonly being shown and can then select the most appropriate ways to train and motivate the athlete to help produce the best performance.

# Topic A.5 Views of personality

## Trait

Studied ☐

Trait views of personality suggest that people have certain characteristics that will determine how they behave. Traits are relatively stable aspects of personality (an individual behaves in a relatively consistent way across a range of situations) and are thought to be inherited. Eysenck said that there were two main dimensions of personality:

- an introversion–extroversion dimension
- a stable–unstable (neurotic) dimension

It is currently thought that trait views may help to explain why athletes choose certain sports but that personality is too simplistic to predict success in a sports situation.

## Situational

Studied ☐

Situational views of personality are different from the trait views, believing that behaviour depends on your situation or environment. These views state that personality is not stable but changes due to our different experiences. It is thought that it is unlikely that someone will behave in the same way in different environments. Situational views think that sports people learn from modelling and copying. Modelling is when people model themselves on people they relate to and look up to. They then begin to watch their role models and copy their behaviour.

## Interactional

Studied ☐

Interactional views of personality believe that in order to predict behaviour you need to look at how the situational and personality traits work together. This view is accepted by most sport psychologists and suggests that when there are strong situational factors, for example, in a penalty shoot out or a short corner, interactional views are more likely to predict the sports person's behaviour than personality traits alone.

## Knowledge recap

1. Give two methods of measuring personality.
2. What is EPI?
3. What is trait behaviour?
4. What is situational behaviour?

# Assessment guidance for learning aim A

## Scenario

For part of your leadership award you have been volunteering as a sports psychologist for a semi-professional sports team. You have been asked to prepare a range of resources that could be used to help improve the team's performance. Your work will need to include information about how personality affects performance.

**2A.P1** **Using relevant examples, describe personality, including methods of measurement and three different views**

**Assessor report:** The command verb in the grading criteria is **describe**. In the learner's answers we would expect to see a detailed account of personality, including methods of measurement and three different views.

## ✍ Learner answer

Personality is the sum of the characteristics that make a person unique.

Personality is made up of lots of different traits or characteristics. It is what makes us, us! Happy, sad, controlled, aggressive or enthusiastic. A football captain needs to be controlled, have leadership qualities, decisive and outgoing to be a good captain.

Personality can be measured by using questionnaires, for example EPI (Eysenck's Personality Inventory), POMS (Profile of Mood States) and carrying out observations, for example observing traits, behaviours. Personality tests and observations can establish if a person is an introvert or extrovert, Type A or Type B, stable or unstable (neurotic). Most sports people will be Type A, these people have the get up and go, they want to be competitive and they want to win. They will probably be extroverts as they want to be with other people, their team mates and are happy with pressure. These people may be stable or unstable and this may depend on the situation they are in.

## Observation

You can measure a sports person's personality and behaviours by observing him or her. A sports coach will watch the performer to see which traits and characteristics the sports person is showing. The coach might look for how the sports person copes with successes and failures, different roles in a sports team and how he or she interacts with other people. These can be recorded for the coach to look over. The coach can identify the performer's strongest and weakest traits.

## Questionnaires

Personality traits and characteristics can be measured by the sports person or the coach by using a questionnaire such as Eysenck's EPI. The questions are easy to complete and all require 'yes' or 'no' answers. The answers are then used to construct a personal profile for the sports person which will indicate the strongest personality traits.

## POMS (Profile of mood states)

This method will show if a performer is in a positive or negative mind set about his or her performance. It is thought that a performer who is positive will perform better than someone who is negative. The sports person's moods (tension, depression, anger, confusion, fatigue and vigour) will be recorded before his or her performance. This will let the sports performer and the coach see where mood is as an indicator of how well the sports person will perform.

Three different views of personality are:

1. **Trait**: relatively consistent way an individual behaves across a range of situations.
   Trait views suggest that personality is made up of a set of traits or characteristics and that these will determine how a person responds and behaves. Examples of traits would be extrovert and introvert, stable and neurotic (unstable). Personalities can be identified as being more towards one end of a scale than another, for example someone will be more extroverted than introverted and more stable than neurotic.
2. **Situational**: how behaviour is determined mainly by the environment.
3. **Interactional**: considers both the individual's traits and the situation he finds himself in when determining behaviour.

The different views help us to get an idea of personality and to predict what a person will do in a sports situation.

**Assessor report:** The learner has briefly described personality. He or she has described methods of measurement in great detail and has produced some description of the trait views. To achieve 2A.P1 the learner needs to describe in much more detail situational and interactional views. The learner must include relevant examples for methods of measuring personality and the three different views to show that he or she understands the topic and can identify how it is applied in a sports situation.

## Assessor report – overall

### What is good about this assessment evidence?

The learner has provided a definition of personality and has given an example. Methods to measure personality have been described and three different views have been mentioned, one with a good level of description.

### What could be improved about this assessment evidence?

The learner has not included enough description for all areas of the criteria. Some of the work lacks depth. To achieve 2A.P1 the learner could improve the description of how personality is measured by giving examples of the types of results you might expect to see from a team player or an individual athlete. To complete the answer on the three different views of personality, the learner should give a sports example to show how each view is interpreted.

## 2A.M1 Explain three different views of personality and how personality can affect sports performance

**Assessor report:** The command verb in the grading criteria is **explain**. In the learner's answers we would expect to see that the learner has developed the points made for the pass criteria and has provided more detail of three different views of personality, and how personality can affect sports performance.

 **Learner answer**

## What is personality?

Personality is the sum of the characteristics that make a person unique.

Personality is what makes us all different. Personality is what gives us our unique set of traits and makes us respond in particular ways to different situations. Personality is a pattern of traits or characteristics which determine our behaviour.

## Different views of personality

Interactional views state that personality is a combination of traits or characteristics and the environment.

This is the most commonly accepted view by sport psychologists to explain behaviour. This view suggests that when situational or environmental factors are strong, they are more likely to predict behaviour than personality traits. For example, if a long distance runner who is an introvert, normally shy and quiet, wins an important race he may run around the track screaming and shouting because he has won the race.

This view believes that people are influenced by the sports situation, the event, the environment and their previous experiences. A sports person who has successfully attempted a new skill will be keen to try it again in a different situation. Someone who has had little luck with a particular skill and has experienced it failing will be less likely to try it in a competition.

## How personality can affect sports performance

To succeed in sport, the athletes' coach must treat every athlete differently, depending on each person's personality.

Each athlete needs to know and understand his or her own personality and traits to prevent this from decreasing performance and be able to overcome any negative personality traits. The coach and the athlete need to be able to control the athlete's mood and arousal levels depending on the situation, level of competition or environment.

A sports coach needs to know if the athlete suffers from anxiety, becomes stressed and worried before a competition, so that this can be dealt with and not affect performance. The sports coach needs to know if the athlete is an extrovert or an introvert. If an extrovert, he or she will enjoy being with other people and will enjoy high pressure situations. If the coach decides that this athlete should train alone and with no-one watching, this may destroy the athlete. He needs to be with other people and he enjoys showing others what he can do. Therefore it is imperative that the coach knows the athlete's personality type so the training is suitable. Another example might be that a football manager plays a more introverted player out of position, and because he is not used to being there, he may play badly; this may also decrease his own motivation and view of his performance.

To be able to predict a sports person's behaviour in any sporting situation, the coach will help him or her to see how the personality traits and the 'situation' work together.

**Assessor report:** The learner has explained only one view of personality, and how personality can affect sports performance. To achieve the 2A.M1 criteria the answer will need to explain another two views with examples of how personality can affect sports performance.

## Assessor report – overall

**What is good about this assessment evidence?**

The learner has successfully explained one view (interactional) of personality and has explained the affect personality can have on sports performance. The correct information has been used throughout the work and the learner has provided suitable sports examples.

**What could be improved about this assessment evidence?**

To achieve the 2A.M1 criteria the learner needs to complete the piece of work. Three views of personality (including trait and situational) need to be fully explained with sports examples. The learner has helped explain the discussions with sports examples which have demonstrated a good level of understanding and application.

## 2A.D1 Analyse three different views of personality and how personality can affect sports performance

**Assessor report:** The command verb in the grading criteria is **analyse**. In a learner's answer we would expect to see the learner identify three different views of personality and several relevant factors of how personality can affect sports performance. The learner should show how they are linked and explain the importance of each.

 **Learner answer**

### Trait views of personality

Personality traits or features of our character are what make us all different and unique. We all have a different set of personality traits. Our different traits affect how we perform in sports, the influence we have over other people and how we respond to situations.

It may be thought that a quiet person would be quiet in all situations and that an outgoing person would be loud all the time. But this is not always the case. A team player who enjoys being with other people and loves the pressure of performing against other 'better' teams may respond very quietly to losing a game. Instead of his normal outgoing, loud, happy to be around other people behaviour, he may want to be alone and not talk to others. This may be because of a previous event when he was in a losing team – he has displayed the same behaviour again.

Different personality traits may give a sports performer an advantage in the chosen sport. An extrovert is usually loud, outgoing, a team player. This will give him an advantage when playing team sports. He will want to be part of a team and enjoy doing things together. He will thrive on the pressure of playing in a game where the situation can change at any time and will perform better for it. For example, a rugby player enjoys the pressure of a player tackling him and the uncertainty of a pass being successful or of a kick going where he wanted it to without being intercepted. An introvert will prefer to be on his own and to compete in sports where the skills are repeated and there is little chance of him being interrupted, and where the environment is unlikely to change. For example, a long distance runner will enjoy running on his own, the continuous pace of running and the fact that the environment stays the same. If we change the rugby player and the long distance runner's places, they would be out of their comfort zones and would probably perform much worse than they really could.

We have dominant personality traits but our behaviour is affected by the environment and our past experiences. For example, if a basketball player knows he can do a perfect lay-up, he has practised it in training on his own and with a defender, he will be very likely to try lay-ups in competition. He will have the confidence that he can do it because he has done it before. Someone who has practised lay-ups and missed them every time may have become frustrated with trying to learn the skill and given up, thinking he can't do it. This person is very unlikely to try a lay-up even if there are no defenders near and he has the ball and enough time. He has had previous negative experiences which have changed his behaviour from a positive one to a negative one.

Overall the trait views suggest that extroverts may become bored easily and are not good at tasks which need concentration, they like to be excited and to do new and different things.

Introverts do not look for excitement and prefer to be in quiet environments and they do like tasks which require concentration and do not like to be distracted. It has been suggested that extroverts are more successful in sports because they cope better with the excitement and tension of competitions and performing. Stable personality types are thought to be more easy-going and stable, less likely to flare up and shout or start an argument. Neurotic or unstable personality types are thought to be more excitable and can become highly aroused. In reality trait views are not realistic and cannot predict the success of a sports person, but they can be used to help indicate personality types and the likeliness of how a person responds in a given situation. This can help the performer and the coach to manage behaviour so that it limits the negative effects on performance.

**Assessor report:** The learner has explained only one view (trait) of personality, and has analysed how personality can affect sports performance in relation to trait views. To achieve the 2A.D1 criteria another two views need to be analysed, with examples of how personality affects sports performance.

## Assessor report – overall

**What is good about this assessment evidence?**

The learner has analysed trait personality views and has provided some good examples of how personality can affect sports performance. The learner has made a good start on this piece of work and has provided some sound analysis of trait views linked to sports performance.

**What could be improved about this assessment evidence?**

The learner needs to complete the piece of work to be able to achieve the criteria. An analysis of interactional and situational views of personality needs to be included. The learner could make more reference to how personality affects performance. Some mention of introverts and extroverts within a sporting context has been made, but this could be expanded to fulfil the analysis criteria of 2A.D1. The learner can use research text as long as this is properly referenced, this may help in the development of the analysis. The learner could try to explain how the same sports person may react to different situations and why, how personality helps to determine behaviour in different sports situations.

# Learning aim B
## Explore the influence that motivation and self-confidence have on sports performance

### Assessment criteria

**2B.P2**   Describe types and views of motivation and the benefits motivation and self-confidence have on sports performance.

**2B.P3**   Summarise, with relevant examples, methods to increase self-confidence in sport.

**2B.P4**   Describe, using relevant examples, factors that influence self-efficacy in sport.

**2B.P5**   Describe goal setting, different types of goals that can be set, and how these can influence sports performance and motivation.

**2B.M3**   Discuss how goal setting can influence motivation and the roles of the different types of goals that can be set.

## Topic B.1 Definition of motivation

Motivation is the internal mechanisms and external stimuli that arouse and direct behaviour. This means that motivation is what gets you to react to something and display particular behaviours. A sports person may be motivated to go to training in order to improve his or her skills in the hope of being picked for the first team.

Figure 2.1 The photograph shows an example of what could motivate a sports person.

# Topic B.2 Types of motivation

## Intrinsic

Figure 2.2 Intrinsic motivation comes from enjoyment of a sport

Intrinsic motivation comes from internal factors, from your own enjoyment of taking part in a sport. You take part in a sport or activity because it is fun and it gives you a great deal of personal satisfaction. For example, someone might choose to take up playing badminton recreationally because they enjoy playing, they find it fun and take pleasure from learning the rules of the sport.

## Extrinsic

Figure 2.3 Extrinsic motivation can come from winning

Extrinsic motivation comes from external factors, from rewards like money, grades, trophies and medals. You take part in a sport or activity because of the threat of punishment if you do not take part or the desire to win and beat others. For example, a swimmer might train for five hours a day every day so that she can perfect her skills and improve her performance because she has a competition coming up and wants to beat the other competitors and win the gold medal.

# Topic B.3 Views of motivation

## Trait centred

Studied ☐

Trait centred views of motivation look at motivation as being a function of an individual's personality, needs and goals. These views are thought to be the most permanent parts of our personality (an example of a trait is determination). An example of this would be an extrovert who is happier playing in a team rather than on his own or an introvert who prefers to compete as an individual and not have to be exposed to the pressure of playing as part of a team.

## Situation centred

Studied ☐

Situational centred views of motivation see motivation as being determined by the situation. Every sports event has its own different situational factors depending on the activity. The event might be for teams or individuals, there may be a prize or it might be just for fun, it may be a national competition or a local tournament. A sports person's motivation will be affected by the situation, for example, a canoeist may be more motivated to do well in a national competition where he could get the chance to be selected for the GB squad than he would if it were a training session – the situations are different and his motivation is determined by the situation.

## Interactional

Studied ☐

Interactional motivation views state that motivation is the result of an interaction between the individual and her environment. These views agree that motivation is affected by both traits and situational factors. An example would be that a highly motivated netball player might be bored with training because the coach does the same things every session, she trains at the same sports centre and uses the same drills. The netballer may have a very motivated personality but because the situation is not interesting to her, she becomes demotivated.

## Topic B.4 Definition of achievement motivation

Achievement motivation is an individual's effort to master or learn a new task, to achieve excellence, to overcome obstacles and to perform better than others. This is our need to achieve, how competitive we are. Our level of achievement motivation will depend on the situation and our personality. An example would be a new cricket player during his first match against another club, his motivation will depend on his perceived chance of winning. He may be prepared to play and see what happens or he may choose not to play.

## Topic B.5 Benefits of motivation on sports performance

There are many benefits of motivation on sports performance. Motivation can decide which sports activity people choose, they may be more motivated to take up a team sport because they enjoy being with other people or take up swimming because they love the water. The effort and intensity a performer puts into his performance depends on his motivation, if he is determined to do well, however much effort is needed, he will perform better. In the face of adversity, when the football team are losing 2-0, motivation can make the players try harder and overcome the score to get more goals and win the game.

## Knowledge recap

1. What is motivation?

2. What is intrinsic motivation?

3. What is extrinsic motivation?

4. What are trait centred views of motivation?

5. What are situation centred views of motivation?

6. What are interactional views of motivation?

7. What is achievement motivation?

8. How can motivation benefit sports performance?

## Topic B.6 Principles of setting goals to increase and direct motivation

The aim of goal setting is to increase and direct a sports person's motivation. For goal setting to be most effective, the goals should be SMARTER.

**S** Specific: the goal must be specific to the sports person; it should state what the person needs to do.

**M** Measureable: the goal needs to be quantifiable; the sports person needs to be able to measure what he has done so that he can see any improvement.

**A** Achievable: the goal must be something that the sports person can actually do. Winning an Olympic gold medal would not be achievable for a 10-year-old who has been to three hockey training sessions.

**R** Realistic: the goal needs to be something the sports person can do. Training for six hours a day is not realistic for someone who is at school all day.

**T** Time-related: the goal needs to have a time frame so that the sports person knows the deadline for achieving the goal.

**E** Exciting: the goal must be exciting or the sports person will get bored and not want to carry on.

**R** Recorded: the goal must be recorded so that the sports person can refer back to it, can see what the goals are and that these are not changing.

By using SMARTER goals a sports person will be able to increase motivation and overall performance.

## Knowledge recap

**1.** What is a SMARTER goal?

## Topic B.7 Definition of self-confidence

Self-confidence is the belief that a desired behaviour can be performed. This is a positive attitude. Sports people with high levels of self-confidence also have higher levels of motivation. For example, a sports person who is very good at a particular sport will usually have the self-confidence to try other sports and be good at them too. The sports person will believe in her own ability and be able to pick up new sports quickly.

## Topic B.8 Benefits of self-confidence

There are many benefits of self-confidence. A positive attitude of self-belief can enable a sports person to produce positive emotion: for example, losing can make that person turn around and look at the situation in a positive way which can help with motivation and enable the person to go on to win. Self-confidence can help to improve concentration and effort: if a sports person is able to concentrate and if more effort is put in, performance will be better. Self-confidence can also help someone to develop positive game plans. The sports person knows she has the skills to be able to go on and win, all that is needed is the opportunities to use those skills. A game plan can help to highlight when skills can be used for the sports person to be able to show what she can do.

## Topic B.9 Methods to increase self-confidence

There are several ways to increase self-confidence. Self-talk is when you talk to yourself in a positive way, you tell yourself that you will be successful. The aim of self-talk is to convince yourself that you can perform well. This can be done. If a cyclist is performing badly and being overtaken by other competitors, she can start saying to herself 'remember your last race when you beat these other cyclists, and you won'. This positive thinking and self-talk will help her to concentrate on a successful performance and help her to go on to win.

Imagery is used by a performer to recreate successful times: the sports person recreates a confident time, imagining herself acting confidently and imagining herself performing successfully. To use imagery an athlete needs to think about a time when she performed successfully. She needs to visualise herself winning and performing well and remember how she performed her skills. She now needs to try to copy the presence she has visualised. This method can help an athlete to improve her skills and overall performance.

## Knowledge recap

1. What is self-confidence?
2. Name two benefits of self-confidence.
3. Name two methods to increase self-confidence.

## Topic B.10 Definition of self-efficacy

Self-efficacy is a person's self-confidence in a specific situation. For sports people this means the amount of self-confidence in their performance in a specific situation. A performer with a high level of self-efficacy will perform well and show good levels of motivation and perseverance. Someone with low self-efficacy will have low expectations and will be unhappy about performing. An elite athlete with years of practice behind her will be keen to use different skills in any situation and be keen to show what she can do, confident in her own ability, displaying a high level of self-efficacy. A novice sports performer who has low self-efficacy may be happy to perform her skills in training but may not want to play as part of a team as she doubts her own ability.

Figure 2.4 It takes self-confidence to achieve a goal

## Topic B.11 Factors affecting self-efficacy

There are four factors which influence self-efficacy: performance accomplishments, vicarious experience, verbal persuasion and imaginal experience.

### Performance accomplishments

Studied ☐

Performance accomplishments allow a sports person to gain confidence from successful previous experiences. When you have experienced success you are more likely to develop high levels of confidence; this will make you keen to repeat the skill or activity again. In training your coach might not let you finish on a bad skill or practice; this is because they want you to be able to remember when you did it right and how it felt to be able to do the skill or practice. For example, when practising back drops on the trampoline the coach may say you will do two more, but you might actually do three if your second attempt was not successful.

## Vicarious experiences

Studied

Vicarious experiences are learnt from watching other sports people performing successfully. By watching a role model demonstrate a skill correctly, you will feel that you will be able to copy her and perform the skill or activity just as well as she does. The role model or significant other should be someone who has a similar ability to the sports performer for this to increase the performer's confidence. For example, if a new wheelchair basketball player sees one of the team who is similar in age and ability perform a successful set shot, she will think that there is no reason why she cannot do it herself and it will help to increase her confidence.

## Verbal persuasion

Studied

Verbal persuasion comes from other people: teachers, coaches and peers can tell you that your performance went well and this will help to increase your confidence in your ability. For example, if a gymnast performs a floor routine and is unsure that she performed well, her coach may say, 'You did really well, you executed each skill with precision and your routine was a success' and the performer will gain confidence in her ability from the feedback.

## Imaginal experiences

Studied

Imaginal experiences help a performer to increase in confidence by imagining performances which were successful. By remembering times when she performed well, the sports person will believe that she can do it again and grow in confidence.

## Knowledge recap

1. What is self-efficacy?

2. What is vicarious experience?

3. Who can give a performer verbal persuasion?

4. What are imaginal experiences?

# Topic B.12 Goals

There are three types of goals: outcome, performance and process goals.

## Outcome goals

Studied ▢

Outcome goals are the result of an event, for example, whether you won or lost the match. Outcome goals are not the best goals for motivating someone when the goal relies on the opposition as well as the performer. A runner might run his personal best in a race, but is still too slow to win the race: this can negatively affect motivation even though he has recorded a personal best. This type of goal can really help improve motivation in the short-term. If you think about someone you really want to beat, it can motivate you to play better.

## Performance goals

Studied ▢

Performance goals look at the athlete's performance. They compare the athlete's current performance against previous ones. These goals are not affected by the performance of others. This means the athlete has more control over his goal and it gives him more motivation. For example, a volleyball player might set a goal of improving their successful serves from 65 per cent to 80 per cent.

## Process goals

Studied ▢

Process goals are what a sports person needs to do to improve his performance. This type of goal is very good for increasing motivation as it gives the performer specific focus; this helps to improve learning and skill development. For example, a swimmer might make it a goal to improve his leg kick by making sure that he kicks from the hip and not the knee. The swimmer knows exactly what he needs to focus on and can learn to do the leg kick correctly to help develop and improve his skill and overall performance.

It is thought that goals are most successful when they use a mixture of these three types. There should be a progression from short-term goals to long-term goals to help increase and maintain the performer's motivation and skill development.

## Topic B.13 Influence of goal setting on sports performance

Goal setting can help to direct attention to certain aspects or areas of performance. It can highlight areas of strength and weakness which can then be identified and improved. For example, if a tennis player's successful volleying return rate is only 20 per cent this can be identified as a goal. The goal could be to improve the tennis player's volleying rate from 20 per cent to 50 per cent. The performer will now spend extra time on this area of the sport, giving it extra attention to ensure that this goal is met.

Mobilising effort means that a sports person can see where she needs to pay more attention and what she needs to put more effort into. It can help motivate her to try harder. This might mean attending more training sessions or spending a longer time in each training session. The sports person's goal may be to spend three nights a week training instead of just one.

Prolonging persistence means that goal setting can help a performer stay focussed for a longer period of time. The season the performer competes in might be 8 months long which is a long time to stay motivated. If the goal is to maintain fitness and to keep winning matches, this will help the performer to stay focussed and help to keep performance at a high standard.

Goal setting can help an individual or sports team to develop new strategies. The goal might be to try different set pieces in training and to use them at least once in a game. This keeps the sports person motivated because she is able to try new things in the event and it keeps her interested and wanting to perform.

## Topic B.14 Influence of goal setting on motivation

Motivation can be hugely improved by goal setting. It can provide a direction for a sports person's behaviour and it can help to maintain focus. The result of goal setting will be that motivation is increased, the sports person is more enthusiastic and committed to training and the outcome will be that overall performance increases.

## Knowledge recap

1. Name two different types of goals.
2. How can goal setting affect performance?
3. How can goal setting affect motivation?

# Assessment guidance for learning aim B

## Scenario

As a sports player you are always looking for ways to improve your performance. Being motivated and self-confident are important traits or characteristics needed by sports people at all levels. Your coach has asked you to produce some material to help improve your motivation and self-confidence. This material could be in the form of a leaflet or a handbook.

### 2B.P2 Describe types and views of motivation and the benefits motivation and self-confidence have on sports performance

**Assessor report:** The command verb in the grading criteria is **describe**. In learners' answers, to meet the 'describe' criteria, we would expect to see a detailed account of the types and views of motivation and the benefits motivation and self-confidence have on sports performance.

See student answer opposite.

**Assessor report:** The learner has identified the types of motivation and the benefits of motivation to sports performance, and has also described one of the views of motivation – trait centred. To achieve 2B.P2 the learner needs to provide further detail to the answer.

## Assessor report – overall

**What is good about this assessment evidence?**

The learner has produced a spider diagram which shows the types and views of motivation and the benefits of motivation. The learner has presented the answer clearly and logically. The learner has produced a good description of trait-centred motivation.

**What could be improved about this assessment evidence?**

To achieve the criteria for 2B.P2 the learner needs to complete the piece of work. The learner should include descriptions of situation and interactional views of motivation in as much detail as has been provided for trait views. The learner must also describe the effects self-confidence can have on sports performance. The learner could develop the answer to include examples of how a sports person uses different types of motivation to improve performance.

## ✍️ Learner answer

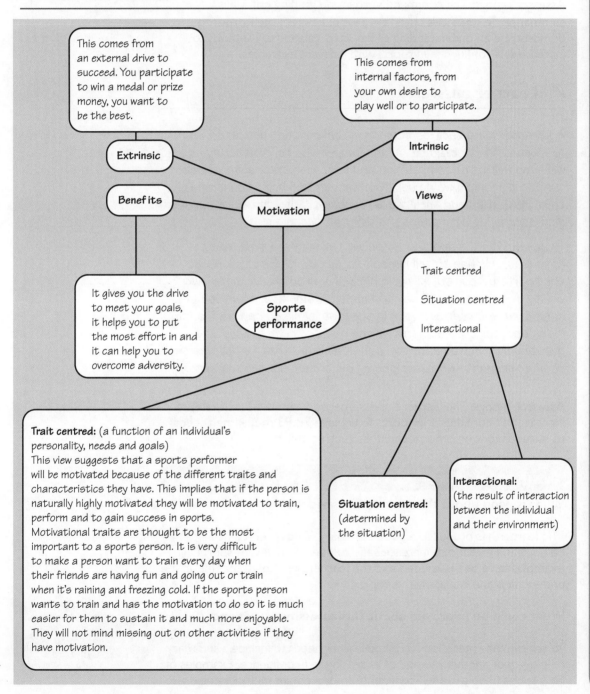

This comes from an external drive to succeed. You participate to win a medal or prize money, you want to be the best.

This comes from internal factors, from your own desire to play well or to participate.

**Extrinsic**

**Intrinsic**

**Benefits**

**Motivation**

**Views**

It gives you the drive to meet your goals, it helps you to put the most effort in and it can help you to overcome adversity.

**Sports performance**

Trait centred

Situation centred

Interactional

**Trait centred:** (a function of an individual's personality, needs and goals)
This view suggests that a sports performer will be motivated because of the different traits and characteristics they have. This implies that if the person is naturally highly motivated they will be motivated to train, perform and to gain success in sports.
Motivational traits are thought to be the most important to a sports person. It is very difficult to make a person want to train every day when their friends are having fun and going out or train when it's raining and freezing cold. If the sports person wants to train and has the motivation to do so it is much easier for them to sustain it and much more enjoyable. They will not mind missing out on other activities if they have motivation.

**Situation centred:** (determined by the situation)

**Interactional:** (the result of interaction between the individual and their environment)

# Summarise, with relevant examples, methods to increase self-confidence in sport

**Assessor report:** The command verb in the grading criteria is **summarise**. To meet this criteria we would expect the learner to demonstrate an understanding of key facts relating to methods to increase self-confidence in sport, with relevant examples.

## ✍ Learner answer

A person who has self-confidence will believe that he can do what he intends to. For example, a long jumper who believes today he will jump well in the competition and beat his personal best. Self-confident people have a positive attitude; this helps to increase their motivation and their overall success. Self-confidence can be increased by using imagery and self-talk techniques.

To use self-talk, a sports person will take himself to a quiet, calm place. He has to tell himself he 'can do it'. Self-talk needs the sports person to believe in himself and to believe in his own ability. A sprinter might say to himself, 'Remember when you last competed, you beat everyone in the last 10m, you can do it again'. If the sprinter uses self-talk during his race he may keep saying over and over in his head, 'You can do this' so that he believes the positive thoughts and uses them to increase his performance.

**Assessor report:** The learner has summarised a method (self-talk) to increase self-confidence in sport. To achieve 2B.P3 the learner needs to include work on other techniques such as imagery.

## Assessor report – overall

**What is good about this assessment evidence?**

The learner has produced a good summary of how self-talk can be used as a method to increase self-confidence. Relevant sports examples have been included and the learner has shown that he or she understands and can apply this topic.

**What could be improved about this assessment evidence?**

To achieve the criteria for 2B.P3 the learner needs to include a summary of imagery or another method of increasing self-confidence. Examples of how sports people use self-confidence improvement methods could also be provided, for example, how an F1 driver may use self-talk to increase performance.

**2B.P4** **Describe, using relevant examples, factors that influence self-efficacy in sport**

**Assessor report:** The command verb in the grading criteria is **describe**. In the learner's answer we would expect to see a detailed account, using relevant examples of the factors that influence self-efficacy in sport.

## Scenario

As a sports player you are always looking for ways to improve your performance. Being motivated and self-confident are important traits or characteristics needed by sports people at all levels. Your coach has asked you to produce some material to help improve your self-efficacy. This material could be in the form of a leaflet or a handbook.

 **Learner answer**

## Factors that influence self-efficacy in sport

| Factors | Sports example |
|---|---|
| Performance accomplishments | By competing in hockey previously and winning some games, a hockey player will gain confidence. She will think that she has won before so she can win again. These performance accomplishments help the hockey player to increase her confidence levels and therefore her self-efficacy level will increase. This will result in a more confident hockey performance and may help to contribute to her team winning more games. |
| Verbal persuasion | Your teachers, coaches and peers play a very important part in your sports development. If they say you are doing well you are going to believe them and this will raise your confidence and self-efficacy. If you have played in a football team against a very good team and lost 1-0, your coach might tell you that you played very well, your defence was tight and you made several effective tackles. This will help you to believe that the next time you play you can win, you have been told your strengths and you now believe that these are good and that your performance can be excellent. Your confidence will grow, increasing your self-efficacy. Instead of being scared to play in the next match, you know you have the ability and will be confident to go out and win. |
| Imaginal experiences | By remembering and imagining times when you played really well and you performed all of your skills correctly, you will increase your self-confidence and your performance will increase. When I am getting ready for a tennis match I remember all of the games I have won, I imagine serving correctly, I remember my forehand returns beating the other player, I think about how I placed the opponent around the court, keeping them off centre and managing to win points against them. This helps me to believe in myself and my confidence grows, I can then go out and win. |

**Assessor report:** The learner has described three factors which influence self-efficacy in sport and has included relevant examples to illustrate the answer. To achieve 2B.P4 the learner needs to include the fourth factor, vicarious experiences, to complete this piece of work.

## Assessor report – overall

**What is good about this assessment evidence?**

The learner has produced a good piece of work, describing three of the four factors which influence self-efficacy in sport and including sports examples. The learner has included examples from his or her own experiences and this shows a good level of understanding. The learner has interpreted the factors and been able to put them into his or her own words with mention of personal experiences.

**What could be improved about this assessment evidence?**

To achieve the criteria for 2B.P4 learner needs to include a description of how vicarious experiences can influence self-efficacy. To develop this piece of work the learner could include more detail about personal experiences. It was good to see reference to how these factors had been used to improve the learner's own confidence and helped with improved performance. It would be very good to see the learner include more information on the personal experiences as examples as this helps the learner to better understand the topic and then be able to use these factors to help improve his or her overall sports performance.

(2B.P5) **Describe goal setting, different types of goals that can be set, and how these can influence sports performance and motivation**

**Assessor report:** The command verb in the grading criteria is **describe**. In a learner's answer we would expect to see a detailed account of goal setting, the different types of goals that can be set, and how these can influence sports performance and motivation.

## Scenario

As a sports player you are always looking for ways to improve your performance. Being motivated and self-confident are important traits or characteristics needed by sports people at all levels. Your coach has asked you to produce some material to help improve you to begin to use goal setting and to be able to help others begin goal setting. This material could be in the form of a leaflet or a handbook.

✍ **Learner answer**

This is how I would use SMARTER to set a goal for Suzi, a Year 10 school team netball player:

| SMARTER | GOAL | How the goal affects performance and motivation |
|---|---|---|
| SPECIFIC | Increase your goal shooting success rate from 55 per cent to 70 per cent. | By performing better and having more success in a skill, Suzi's overall performance and motivation will increase. She will want to shoot goals because she is getting better at it and the more practice she has, the better her performance gets. She will become more motivated and do even more practice, a win-win situation for Suzi! |
| MEASUREABLE | Goals scored and missed will be recorded during each match and practice session. | |
| ACHIEVABLE | Suzi is a shooter and has been playing this position for two years. | Because the goal is something Suzi can do, it is achievable. This will help to increase her motivation. If we gave her a goal which she could not complete, it would lead to her becoming demotivated. Again, if the goal is too easy she will not be motivated and her performance will not increase. Because this is a goal she can complete, Suzi will want to do it, she will be motivated to do it and her performance will increase as she gets more and more skilled at shooting. |

| REALISTIC | I have increased her goal success rate by 15 per cent – this is something Suzi should be able to do. | |
| --- | --- | --- |
| TIME-RELATED | The goal will begin on 10 Sept 2012 and end on 9 Dec 2012. | |
| EXCITING | Suzi loves shooting in netball and wants to be better; this goal is something she will want to do. | |
| RECORDED | I will keep a copy of the goal and give Suzi a copy. | |

The three types of goals are outcome, performance and process goals. Suzi's goal is a mixture of all three. This goal will make Suzi more motivated and will help to increase her overall performance.

**Assessor report:** The learner has identified how he or she would use goal setting to increase motivation and performance. To achieve 2B.P5 the learner would need to describe the missing goal types and how they can affect motivation and sports performance.

## Assessor report – overall

**What is good about this assessment evidence?**

The learner has produced a table to show how he or she would apply SMARTER to make a goal for a sports person. The learner has provided some background about the sports person, her age and ability. The learner has used this information to produce a SMARTER goal which would be suitable for the sports person and has also described some of the types of goals, specific and achievable.

**What could be improved about this assessment evidence?**

To achieve the criteria for 2B.P5 the learner needs to describe all of the different types of SMARTER goals and how these can influence sports performance and motivation. The learner has demonstrated a full understanding of goal setting and can apply the theory to a real situation. However, some goal types have been omitted and so the criteria have not been fulfilled. To achieve the 2B.P5 criteria the learner could also describe the three different types of goal: outcome, performance and process goals. This could be done with a sports example to support the descriptions. The learner should also include more description of how sports performance and motivation can be increased by using goal setting. The learner has attempted to mention that Suzi's motivation would increase because she loves netball.

## 2B.M3 Discuss how goal setting can influence motivation and the roles of the different types of goals that can be set

**Assessor report:** The command verb in the grading criteria is **discuss**. In the answers we would expect to see that the learner had examined and commented on how goal setting can influence motivation and the roles of the different types of goals that can be set.

 **Learner answer**

### The three different types of goals: outcome, performance and process goals.

Outcome goals rely on the outcome of an event. These goals do not always work the best at motivating someone. For example, we might give an archer a goal to hit the yellow ring (bull's eye) twice in his next competition. This makes him feel really good as he thinks this is something he can achieve, so his motivation increases. But on the day of his competition all of the competitors score two or more bull's eyes and he does too. But this makes him feel really let down. He feels demotivated now – if everyone can do it and beat his target, it was not a very good target and it makes him think his performance was poor, even though for him two bull's eyes was excellent and showed that his performance had improved.

Because outcome goals compare an individual's performance to the end result and to that of others' performance, they can often be demotivating. Outcome goals do not look at the actual performance, whether the technique was carried out correctly or whether the performer has performed efficiently and effectively. They simply identify where the performer has come in relation to others. If a performer is repeatedly unsuccessful, this type of goal can be catastrophic to performance. The performer will no longer believe in himself, he will lose self-confidence and self-efficacy and lose his motivation. The goal will have done the total opposite of what it was intended to do. However, if the performer meets an outcome goal, comes first in a race, beats all other competitors, then it has been a useful tool and could be used again. But there may come a time when the athlete has performed so well, not only won the race but won by a large difference, that the goal does not recognise the achievement he has made, so the goal could then become de-motivating. Performance and process goals may be better at motivating a performer, particularly if the goals are to be used long-term.

Process goals identify what a sports person needs to do to improve performance. These goals can really help to increase a person's motivation. The goal looks at improving skills by making the sports person spend more time learning how to do the skill and developing his own performance. For example, we could give a rugby player a goal to increase his passing skills. We would explain to the player why this skill is important and show him how to perform the skill perfectly. We can then get the rugby player practising. To make it more difficult we can add running to the pass, so that he has to pass on the move and then we can add a defender so that he has to pass around another player with accuracy. During the process of meeting this goal, the player is learning how to perform the skill correctly and how to use it successfully in a pressurised situation. This will help to increase his motivation as he knows he can do the skill and repeat it in other situations. His performance will therefore increase.

**Assessor report:** The learner has discussed how goal setting can influence motivation and the roles of the different types of goal that can be set, by fully discussing outcome goals. However, the leaner has not completed this piece of work. To achieve 2B.M3 the learner needs to include a discussion of performance and process goals and how they can affect motivation.

## Assessor report – overall

**What is good about this assessment evidence?**

Within the discussion of the types of goals, the leaner has included examples as to how goal setting can influence motivation. The learner has included relevant sports examples to illustrate process and outcome goals. The learner has made some sound comments about the use of the types of goal and how they can affect a sports performer's motivation both positively and negatively.

**What could be improved about this assessment evidence?**

To achieve the criteria for 2B.M3 the learner needs to include a completed discussion of how performance and process goals can affect motivation. The learner should provide equal detail for the discussions of all three types of goals. The piece of work could be completed in the same style as the discussion about outcome goals.

The learner should identify the benefits and negatives of each type of goal. It would be interesting for the learner to use examples of goals and types of goals that he or she has used and how these affected his or her own motivation and performance.

## 2B.M2 Discuss the benefits motivation and self-confidence have on sports performance

**Assessor report:** The command verb in the grading criteria is **discuss**. In the answers we would expect to see that the learner had examined and commented on the benefits motivation and self-confidence have on sports performance.

### Scenario

As a sports player you are always looking for ways to improve your performance. Being motivated and self-confident are important traits or characteristics needed by sports people at all levels. Your coach has asked you to produce some material to help improve your motivation and self-confidence. This material could be in the form of a leaflet or a handbook.

 **Learner answer**

### The benefits of motivation and self-confidence on sports performance

Motivation is what drives us to do something. It can be intrinsic, from inside ourselves – we do something because we enjoy it. Extrinsic motivation comes from external forces, the desire to win a medal or prize money. We take part because we want to be the best.

Self-confidence is the positive attitude a person has about their ability to perform something. A sports person who has a high level of self-confidence will believe that they have a high performance level and will be motivated to do well.

If someone has the belief in himself that he can win, he will perform better. A person with high levels of motivation will want to go to training sessions and will want to take part actively in every drill. This person's skills and ability level will increase; this is because he is spending so much time refining his skills. Because the person's skills are better, his self-confidence will increase, he knows he can do the skills and can win when he competes. This then makes the person more and more motivated and the more he wants to train and compete, the better he will get and the more success he will see.

If a sports person is a little nervous about training, if he is not sure that he will be able to do what is asked of him, he is scared of showing himself up and failing. This person is likely to want to skip training sessions, he is not motivated because he thinks he is no good. Because he misses training sessions, his skill level does not improve, his confidence is low because he is unable to perform skills others of the same ability can. He will lose more motivation and confidence because when he competes he is not prepared and will perform badly. It is a vicious cycle.

If a sports person becomes too motivated he may start to over-train. Because he wants to improve and wants to win, he begins to spend more time training and this could lead to over-use injuries and a high risk that he could burn out. Too much motivation can be as dangerous to performance as too little. If we can suggest that motivation and self-confidence are linked and that a performer with a high level of motivation will have a high level of self-confidence, a performer with too much motivation would have too much self-confidence and a performer with a low level of motivation would have a low level of self-confidence. Both the coach and the performer need to be aware of motivation levels and ensure that the performer does not suffer from too high or too low levels of motivation through the entire training and competing year.

**Assessor report:** The learner has produced evidence of a discussion of the benefits motivation and self-confidence can have on sports performance. To achieve 2B.M2 the learner needs to include more detail about the disadvantages of motivation; there should be an equal amount of discussion examining the benefits and negatives of motivation and self-confidence.

## Assessor report – overall

**What is good about this assessment evidence?**

The learner has given a good explanation of motivation and self-confidence. Sports examples have been included and the problems associated with low levels of motivation have been highlighted. The learner has included a sound discussion of the benefits motivation can have on performance.

**What could be improved about this assessment evidence?**

To achieve the criteria for 2B.M2 the learner should examine the benefits of motivation and self-confidence equally – there is more evidence for motivation, the learner has included more discussion about motivation and sports performance. Where the learner has discussed the benefits and weaknesses of motivation and self-confidence, the answer could be expanded to include potential solutions and examples for each scenario. The learner could interview a sports coach and ask how he uses motivational tools, what he sees as an advantage and how he deals with an under-motivated sports person.

## 2B.D2 Analyse the benefits motivation and self-confidence have on sports performance

**Assessor report:** The command verb in the grading criteria is **analyse**. In the answer we would expect to see the learner identify several of the benefits of motivation and self-confidence and the effects they have on sports performance. The learner should show how they are linked and explain the importance of each.

 **Learner answer**

## The benefits of motivation on sports performance

Motivation is a very important key to sports success. It is what gives us the desire to go out and train on a rainy day or compete in our second match of the week. Motivation has two types, intrinsic and extrinsic. Intrinsic motivation comes from inside us. It makes us want to take up a sport and we do it because we want to, because we enjoy it and because we love doing that sport. Extrinsic motivation comes from other sources – it could be that we want to be the youngest, most successful basketball player, or we want to win the £10,000 prize money or we want to beat everyone else and be the best in the world. Motivation is an important drive for a sports person, but if they are too motivated problems can arise.

### Benefits of motivation

If a sports person is motivated to do well in his sport he will not miss a training session, he will want to play at every opportunity and his performance will be at a high level. The sports person's coach, teacher or peers will be crucial to ensuring that he is highly motivated at all times without him experiencing any problems. A badminton coach will make sure that the player is attending all training sessions. At these sessions they will ensure that the player is putting all his efforts into practising and refining his skills. The coach will enter the player for competitions so that he is competing frequently and is able to improve his performance due to experiencing real, competitive situations. The coach will also make sure that the player is performing at a high level at all times. The coach needs the badminton player to be motivated so that he wants to perform and does so at the very best of his ability.

## Problems with too much motivation

When a sports performer competes at a high level, he can feel a lot of pressure to succeed. This makes the sports person feel that he has to train more often and harder. The sports person thinks that he has to train more in order to increase his performance and do as well as he can. The performer is in danger of becoming too motivated. Over-motivation can lead to the sports person over-training and burning out. This would leave the sports person bored, depressed and performing at a lower level. This can also cause the performer to endure an unnecessary injury. If a performer is over-motivated he may begin to show mood swings and not enjoy what he is doing anymore. Burnout means that the sports person tries harder and harder to meet the demands of his training and competitions, that he starts to fail and becomes unsuccessful, so he tries even harder. When a sports person suffers from burnout he does not want to do the sport anymore and he does not enjoy participating. Unfortunately burnout happens to a lot of young athletes.

Young footballers will enjoy playing professionally, enjoy the training and especially the salary. Then, after a while they may see that they are not improving as much as they had hoped and maybe are not getting selected for the team every week. Then begin to train harder and harder, but still don't see an improvement and notice other players being picked before them. They may start to get bored of having to train every day, they want to do something else instead of train and they lose their love of the game. It is very important the early signs of over-motivation are identified so that the performer does not burn out, injure himself or begin to hate his favourite sport.

## The benefits of self-confidence on sports performance

A performer who has a high level of self-confidence will have a high level of motivation, will believe in his own performance and be confident to go out and show people what he can do. Self-confidence gives a sports performer a positive attitude – he believes he can win, this fuels him on to success. However, self-confidence can be related to a situation. You may find a performer who has high levels of self-confidence in training – he performs well and shows that he can repeat these skills in a competitive situation. But when he enters a competition and performs against others in a new environment, for example, an away football match, he crumbles. This performer had the confidence to perform in front of his peers and coach but when faced with an away team, an away pitch and away fans he cannot cope with the pressure and his performance suffers.

**Assessor report:** The learner has analysed the benefits motivation can have on sports performance. To achieve 2B.D2 the learner needs to provide completed evidence of an analysis of the benefits of self-confidence.

## Assessor report – overall

### What is good about this assessment evidence?

The learner has produced a sound analysis of the benefits of motivation on sports performance. The learner has explained the benefits and problems of motivation and has provided examples throughout the analysis. The learner has shown how over-motivation can have a detrimental effect on sports performance. The learner has included some description of self-confidence and its affect on performance.

### What could be improved about this assessment evidence?

To achieve the criteria for 2B.D2 the learner must include an equal analysis of the benefits of self-confidence on performance. Relevant sports examples should be included and could include personal experiences of training, playing, performance and motivation levels. The learner could include examples of sports people who have struggled with motivation and self-confidence issues, for example, Andy Murray, the British tennis player, who lost his motivation. He began to hate tennis, he did not want to train and did not even want to compete. Andy's performance decreased as a result of this loss of motivation. He spent a lot of time addressing this issue, retrained himself to enjoy tennis, gained some motivation and has gone on to win major events, including the Olympic gold medal for tennis.

# Learning aim C
## Know about arousal and anxiety, and the effects they have on sports performance

### Assessment criteria

**2C.P6** Describe, using relevant examples, different types of anxiety.

**2C.P7** Describe, using four theories, the effect arousal and anxiety have on sports performance and their control.

**2C.M4** Assess, using four theories, the effect arousal and anxiety have on sports performance and their control.

**2C.D3** Evaluate imagery and relaxation techniques as methods of controlling arousal and anxiety, and in improving sports performance.

## Topic C.1 Definition of anxiety

Anxiety is the level of worry or nervousness an individual experiences. This means how much a sports person worries about his performance, his ability, his next competition. Anxiety is negative emotional feelings which are caused by an increase in arousal, usually when the performer is in a high pressure situation, somewhere where he feels stressed and worries he will fail. A diver will feel anxious the first time they step out on to the high board to perform at his first competition.

Figure 3.1 Anxiety can affect performance

# Topic C.2 Types of anxiety

There are four different types of anxiety. State and trait anxiety are involved with your feelings and emotions. Somatic and cognitive anxiety are the physical effects a performer actually experiences.

## State

Studied ☐

State anxiety is a temporary change: you feel tension and apprehension due to your nervous system being activated. A novice baseball player may feel really nervous and apprehensive when she goes out to her first game. Professional runners may actually feel worried before the start of a big race as they feel nervous about where they may place in the event. State anxiety usually goes after the sports person has begun the activity or event and begins to settle into performing.

## Trait

Studied ☐

Trait anxiety is a personality factor: the person with high trait anxiety will feel tense and apprehensive in different situations because her nervous system is constantly being activated. Trait anxiety is something you already have and will affect how you respond to different situations. If a sports person has a high level of trait anxiety she is likely to feel anxious in a wide variety of situations: before a match, trying out a new skill, performing in front of peers. A sports performer with a low level of trait anxiety is likely to be less stressed about whatever situation she is in; she will not mind who is watching or how good the opposition are.

## Somatic (physical effects)

Studied ☐

Somatic anxiety shows itself as physical effects. A sports person may feel butterflies in her stomach before the start of a match, her muscles may tense up as she prepares to perform a skill and her heart rate and breathing rates will increase. Somatic anxiety is how the body responds to high pressured situations. An ice skater may feel sick before the start of her routine, she may be worrying about the success of her performance, and her heart rate and breathing rate actually increase. As she begins to perform, her nerves will normally settle, her heart rate will start to come down as she performs well and focuses on the skating.

## Cognitive (mental effects)

Studied ☐

Cognitive anxiety is the mental or psychological aspects of feeling worried, unable to concentrate and being quick tempered. A sports person worries about how well she will perform before she goes out to her event. The sports person may be unable to concentrate and snap at her coach or other team members because she is worried about performing. This type of anxiety may cause a sports performer to have difficulty concentrating before and even during her performance.

# Topic C.3 How arousal and anxiety affect sports performance

Arousal and anxiety can affect sports performance. There are four theories as to how this relationship takes place.

## Drive theory

Studied ☐

The drive theory states that there is a linear relationship between arousal and performance. It shows that as arousal increases, the sports person's performance improves. For example, a professional basketball player plays well during a match and as the game goes on, he becomes more aroused and 'into' the game and as a result his performance continues to increase.

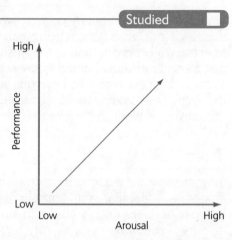

Figure 3.2 Drive theory shows a relationship between arousal and performance

## Inverted U hypothesis

Studied ☐

The inverted U hypothesis suggests that arousal levels and performance increase up to a level, to an optimum point, then they both begin to decrease as arousal becomes too much and performance suffers. For example, a footballer could be playing really well but as time goes on his performance begins to decrease and the more aroused he becomes the worse his performance gets. To perform at the optimum level this theory needs the performer to be aroused enough to perform well but not so aroused that he begins to make mistakes.

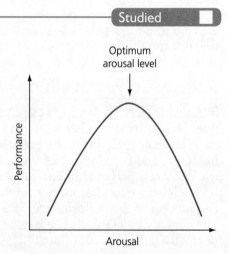

Figure 3.3 The inverted U hypothesis

## Catastrophe theory

The catastrophe theory shows that an increase in cognitive arousal (feelings and thoughts, for example, worry and uncertainty) will improve performance at low levels of physiological arousal (physical effects, for example, increased heart and breathing rate) and that at high levels of physiological arousal, performance will rapidly decrease – a catastrophe. For example, when a rock climber has a low level of arousal, climbing on his practice wall, he will climb well. On a new rock face he may become over-aroused, causing his performance to decrease. The climber needs to take a moment to relax, concentrate on what he is doing and regain his optimum level of arousal or his performance will continue to decrease.

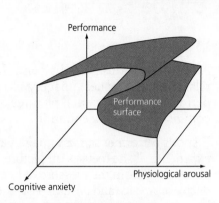

Figure 3.4 Catastrophe theory

## Reversal theory

The reversal theory states that a sports performer can interpret arousal as a factor to increase arousal. A sports performer can interpret high or low arousal levels as pleasant or unpleasant.

The reversal theory uses the following words to describe how a performer might be feeling:

- anxiety (unpleasant high arousal)
- excitement (pleasant high arousal)
- boredom (unpleasant low arousal)
- relaxation (pleasant low arousal)

For example, if a swimmer enjoys being aroused and finds it exciting, he will look forward to becoming aroused and this will make him perform well. A performer who enjoys arousal can use it as a motivational tool to increase performance. If a sports person finds high arousal unpleasant, he will not perform well – he will become too anxious and unable to perform.

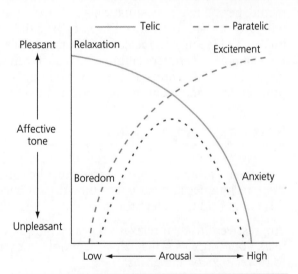

|  | Low arousal | High arousal |
|---|---|---|
| **Telic state** | Relaxation (pleasant) | Anxiety (unpleasant) |
| **Paratelic state** | Boredom (unpleasant) | Excitement (pleasant) |

Figure 3.5 Reversal theory

Learning aim C: Know about arousal and anxiety, and the effects they have on sports performance

# Topic C.4 How anxiety and arousal can be controlled

## Imagery

Studied ☐

Anxiety and arousal can be controlled by using imagery and relaxation techniques. Imagery is a technique where the sports performer creates mental pictures to help reduce stress and increase confidence and concentration.

A sports performer can use imagery by imagining a relaxing experience. If she focuses on pictures in her mind of being in a calm place, away from the pressure of her performance, it can help to decrease anxiety and arousal. For example, if the sports person closes her eyes, thinks about being on the beach, lying in the sand, imagining herself relaxing, she will lower her anxiety and arousal and be able to focus more on her performance and will feel ready to compete.

The sports performer can benefit from imagery by rehearsing a successful performance. It can be used by the sports person to picture herself in a new situation and imagine how her performance will look or to remember feelings of past situations and use these images and feelings to recreate her performance and success. For example, a sprinter can imagine herself running round the track, picturing what her arms and legs were doing, how she ran past the other athletes and went on to be the first over the line.

## Relaxation techniques

Studied ☐

Relaxation techniques help to reduce muscle tension to reduce anxiety and arousal. Sports people must be careful when they use these techniques to ensure that they do not become too relaxed – this could lead to under arousal and a decrease in performance.

Progressive muscular relaxation is a technique where you tense and relax your muscles. This helps the whole body to relax and helps to lower anxiety and arousal.

How to use progressive muscular relaxation:

- Loosen your clothing, take off your shoes, and get comfortable.
- Relax, breathe in and out in slow, deep breaths.
- Start to think about your right foot.
- Tense the muscles in your right foot; hold for a count of 10.
- Relax your right foot. Focus on the tension leaving your foot and the way it feels loose.
- Start to think about your left foot.
- Follow the same pattern of holding your muscles and releasing.
- Move up through your body using the same technique, through your legs, back, stomach, arms and face.

Mind to muscle techniques are also used to reduce anxiety and arousal. A performer thinks about a muscle and feels it working through its range of movement. You need to focus on where the muscle should be contracting and imagine it working to move your body. This technique helps the sports performer to build a mental link with her muscles; this will help to relieve anxiety and arousal and will help the performer to develop her training and performance.

Breathing techniques can be used when a performer starts to feel pressured. When we are anxious we often hold our breath – this can cause muscle tension and actually make us feel worse.

Sports where the performer has breaks are good for using breathing techniques as the performer can relax whilst they are waiting to perform again to help combat anxiety and arousal.

How to use breathing techniques:

- Sit or lie down somewhere comfortable.
- Breathe in through your nose.
- Breathe out through your mouth.
- Push out as much air as you can as you hold in your abdominal muscles.
- Continue to breathe in through your nose and out through your mouth.

## Knowledge recap

1. When might a sports performer feel anxious?

2. What is the difference between trait and state anxiety?

3. What is the difference between somatic and cognitive anxiety?

4. What effect can anxiety have on performance?

5. How does the drive theory link performance to arousal?

6. What is the optimum point in the inverted U theory?

7. What is physiological arousal?

8. How can a sports person control anxiety and arousal?

9. Name two relaxation techniques.

# Assessment guidance for learning aim C

## Scenario

You have been asked to create an information pack by your sports coach, to help you to improve your performance and that of your team mates. You have been studying anxiety and its effect on sports performance at school. Your coach has suggested that you use this information to make a PowerPoint presentation to show your team mates how anxiety can affect performance and how to overcome any negative responses.

### 2C.P6 Describe, using relevant examples, different types of anxiety

**Assessor report:** The command verb in the grading criteria is **describe**. We would expect to see the learner give a detailed account of the different types of anxiety in the answer.

### ✍ Learner answer

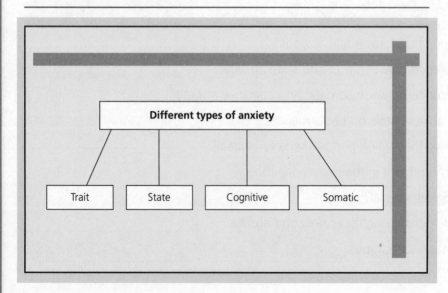

## Trait anxiety

- Trait: a personality factor characterised by stable, consistent feelings of tension and apprehension across many situations due to the nervous system being continually activated.

- Example: a new triple jumper joining a club and attending her first training session. She might have a high level of trait anxiety and be tense and worried about being in this situation.

## State anxiety

- State: temporary, changing feelings of tension and apprehension due to the nervous system becoming activated.

- State anxiety occurs when a performer is in a certain situation, e.g. at the start of a 100 metre race or waiting for the video referee to make a decision in a rugby league game. This anxiety usually decreases when the performer resumes or starts to compete.

- Example: a javelin thrower feeling tense and apprehensive before his event. This is because his nervous system has responded to the situation of him competing by producing worrying feelings.

## State anxiety

- Affects performance.
- Usually occurs before competition or performance.
- Helps the performer to focus on what he is doing; this can increase performance as it allows him to think about what he needs to do and how.
- Can make the performer become too anxious, making him too nervous about competing. This could result in the performer not wanting to perform at all or when he does perform, because he is worried, he will perform badly.

> ## Cognitive
>
> - Cognitive: mental effects, for example, increased feelings of worry, inability to concentrate, quick tempered.
> - Example: a canoeist feels worried before his race. He will be quick tempered and may be unable to concentrate on anything.

> ## Somatic anxiety
>
> - Somatic: physical effects, for example, butterflies in the stomach, muscle tension, increases in heart rate and breathing rate.
> - Example: a gymnast feels butterflies in her tummy and her heart and breathing rate go up before she performs her new routine for the first time in front of her coach.

**Assessor report:** The learner has attempted to describe the different types of anxiety. Sports examples have been included and understanding of this topic has been demonstrated. To achieve the criteria 2C.P6 the learner should describe all the types of anxiety in the same amount of detail used for state anxiety.

## Assessor report – overall

**What is good about this assessment evidence?**

The learner has produced a set of PowerPoint slides. They have identified the four different types of anxiety and have provided a sports specific example for each type of anxiety. The learner has also gone on to further describe state anxiety with relevant sports examples.

**What could be improved about this assessment evidence?**

To achieve the criteria for 2C.P6 the learner needs to include more detail about trait, cognitive and somatic types of anxiety. With their PowerPoint slides the learner should include notes pages; this will allow them to have more room to make their descriptions. The learner could add more detail by describing how different types of anxiety can affect performance in both negative and positive ways, as has been done for state anxiety.

## 2C.P7 Describe, using four theories, the effect arousal and anxiety have on sports performance and their control

**Assessor report:** The command verb in the grading criteria is **describe**. We would expect to see a detailed account of the effect arousal and anxiety have on sports performance and their control, using four theories, in the answer.

## Scenario

You have been asked to create an information pack by your sports coach, to help you to improve your performance and that of your team mates. You have been studying anxiety and its effect on sports performance at school. Your coach has suggested that you use this information to show your team mates how anxiety can affect performance and how to overcome any negative responses.

## ✍ Learner answer

| Theory | Effect of arousal and anxiety on sport |
|---|---|
| **Drive theory:** As a sports person's arousal increases so will performance. | When an elite footballer plays in a match he is aroused, he wants to be there, he wants to play and he wants to win. The footballer's arousal levels will increase. Throughout the match, as the footballer gets more involved with the game, his arousal levels increase and he plays even better. |
| **Inverted U hypothesis:** As a sports person's arousal levels increase, his performance will increase, but only up to an optimal point of arousal, then his performance will decrease. | When a golfer goes out to play a round in a small competition, she will be aroused, her performance will increase and she will play well. As the round goes on she will become more aroused, she will become more competitive and more interested in her own game and what her skills are like. As she becomes more aroused, she reaches an optimum point and her performance is really good. Then she becomes over-aroused, her opponent may have taken the lead and she becomes annoyed, her performance now starts to decrease and as she gets more and more aroused and anxious, her performance gets worse. |

**Assessor report:** The learner has briefly described two theories to show the effect of arousal and anxiety on sports performance and their control. To achieve 2C.P7 the learner needs to describe all four theories

## Assessor report – overall

**What is good about this assessment evidence?**

The learner has produced a table to show the theories of arousal and anxiety and their theoretical effect on performance. The learner has provided sports examples to describe these theories and effects. The learner has interpreted the theories in his or her own words and has come up with realistic examples.

**What could be improved about this assessment evidence?**

To achieve the criteria for 2C.P7 the learner needs to include a description of each of the four theories and give more detail about how anxiety and arousal can affect performance. The learner could improve upon the table by including a column to describe the theory in more detail and then expand upon the sports examples to demonstrate the effects of anxiety and arousal on performance.

## 2C.M4 Assess, using four theories, the effect arousal and anxiety have on sports performance and their control

**Assessor report:** The command verb in the grading criteria is **assess**. In the answer we would expect to see that the learner had evaluated the importance or success of the effect arousal and anxiety have on sports performance and their control, using four theories.

 **Learner answer**

### The effect of arousal and anxiety on sports performance and their control

#### The drive theory

The drive theory suggests that as a sports person becomes aroused, her performance increases.

#### The inverted U theory

The inverted U theory suggests that a sports person becomes aroused and performance increases up to an optimum level. Too little arousal and performance will suffer, the sports person will not be focused enough to play well; too much arousal and performance will decrease.

Arousal can have both a positive and negative effect on sports performance. Both the drive theory and the inverted U theory suggest that a performer needs to become aroused for performance to increase. Under-arousal is just as big a problem as over-arousal. Without arousal, a performer does not have the motivation and enthusiasm to train, play or compete. Too much arousal will cause a sports person to make mistakes, produce the wrong skills and possibly break rules.

By controlling anxiety, a performer can help to reduce the reverse affects it may have on decreasing performance. However, the drive theory suggests that as arousal increases, performance increases. This may be true in an elite athlete who thrives on the pressure of competition and enjoys performing and competing. But for a novice who has never experienced competition and has only practised her skills in training sessions, the pressure and excitement of a competition may be too much and in this case, as arousal increases, performance may decrease.

The inverted U theory supports the idea that a performer needs some arousal to perform well, at an optimum level, and that too much arousal leads to performance being damaged and decreasing. For example, when a horse rider goes out to perform for the first time she needs to be aroused to want to perform; under-arousal may cause her to become too relaxed and not motivated to perform. When she become aroused, her performance increases and as this happens, she reaches an optimum level of performance. It is easy to understand what could happen next. Maybe the horse behaves in a way she had not anticipated, possibly she tries too hard and jumps too early, causing her to fail a jump. These mistakes will be the start of her performance decreasing and as she tries harder to recover, the more mistakes she makes. Too much arousal has caused her performance to decrease. If the horse rider can take a moment to think about what is happening, breathe deeply and try to relax, she may be able to recover her concentration and focus on what she needs to do to increase her performance.

**Assessor report:** The learner has assessed two theories and attempted to evaluate the effect on arousal and anxiety on sports performance and their control. To achieve 2C.M4 the learner needs to complete the evidence by including an evaluation of all four theories and the effects of arousal and anxiety on sports performance.

## Assessor report – overall

**What is good about this assessment evidence?**

The learner has made some good comments about arousal and how the two different theories, inverted U and drive, explain the link between performance and arousal. The learner has provided sports examples to expand the answer. The learner has described the benefits and problems associated with arousal.

**What could be improved about this assessment evidence?**

To achieve the criteria for 2C.M4 the learner needs to include an evaluation/assessment of all four theories and needs to add work about the catastrophe and reversal theories. The learner could develop the evidence further by describing the theories and then using sports examples to say how the theory applies in a sporting situation to the performer and his or her level of arousal. The learner has focused on arousal and has made little reference to anxiety which should be included to achieve the criteria. The learner could add diagrams to support the answer and to help explain how the theories can be used in practice to show how arousal/anxiety affect sports performance and how they can be managed.

## 2C.D3 Evaluate imagery and relaxation techniques as methods of controlling arousal and anxiety, and in improving sports performance

**Assessor report:** The command verb in the grading criteria is **evaluate**. In the answer we would expect to see the learner cover all of the information and make a judgement on the importance of imagery and relaxation techniques as methods of controlling arousal and anxiety to improve sports performance.

### Scenario

You have been asked to create an information pack by your sports coach, to help you to improve your performance and that of your team mates. You have been studying anxiety and its affect on sports performance at school. Your coach has suggested that you use this information to show your team mates how they can control arousal and anxiety by using imagery and relaxation techniques to improve sports performance.

 **Learner answer**

### Imagery as a method of controlling arousal and anxiety and improving sports performance

It is important that the coach and the athlete identify how the performer copes with arousal and how it affects his performance. Imagery and other relaxation techniques can help the performer to lower arousal to a level which allows him to perform at his optimum level.

Arousal is the state of readiness of a sports person to perform a skill or activity; his behaviour will be motivated in a positive or negative way, depending on how he perceives the situation. A sports person aims to have the optimum amount of arousal so that his performance increases and he works at his highest level.

Anxiety is feelings of negative emotions caused by an increase in arousal levels when a sports person is in a high pressured situation.

Arousal has negative and positive effects on performance and controlling it can be a successful tool for a sports performer.

Too little arousal will lead a sports person to be laid back, not too bothered about performing and will not enable him to reach his highest levels of performance. Too much arousal and a performer may become nervous, make mistakes and ultimately his performance will decrease. However, performers can change the way they deal with arousal. If a performer enjoys being aroused and is excited by the pressure of a competition and looks forward to the feelings arousal brings, he can channel this into his performance and will perform at his highest level. If a performer is afraid of arousal and does not like the experiences it brings, it may detract from his performance and he will perform badly.

To use imagery a sports person has to think about an elite athlete in his sport and what he looks like performing. The sports person has to imagine himself doing the same skill and executing it just as perfectly as the elite athlete. This will help the sports person to develop his own skills and help him to improve his performance. Imagery can be used to recreate emotions and experiences and should involve as many senses as possible. To ensure that imagery works as well as it can, the sports person should try to imagine the sounds (if there is a crowd, will they be cheering?), the smells (is the performance outside or inside?), what the situation feels like (will he feel sunlight on his skin or wind through his hair?). All of these feelings can help the performer to recreate a perfect situation and a perfect performance that he can apply to his new scenario.

Imagery can be used in different ways to produce different sensations which can be beneficial to the sports person. The sports person can picture escaping to a calm, quiet place, away from the pressure of the competitive situation. He can recreate the kinaesthetic feelings of successful movements and performance. The sports person may choose to create images of what might happen during his performance and visualise how to deal with them. Or the performer could choose to create emotional feelings that he might feel when performing in a stressful situation, like success and control.

The sports person can experiment with using these four different methods and then select the one which helps him to relax and ensure that he has lowered his anxiety and controlled his arousal, helping him to perform at his highest level.

**Assessor report:** The learner has produced evidence which evaluates imagery as a method to control arousal and anxiety, and improve sports performance. To achieve 2C.D3 the learner needs to fully evaluate relaxation techniques as methods of controlling arousal and anxiety to improve sports performance.

## Assessor report – overall

### What is good about this assessment evidence?

The learner has evaluated how imagery is used and how it can help to control anxiety and arousal. The learner has provided descriptions of anxiety and arousal. Sports examples have been provided and the learner has explained in his or her own words how arousal can be a positive and negative force in increasing sports performance.

### What could be improved about this assessment evidence?

To achieve the criteria for 2C.D3 the learner needs to provide a thorough evaluation of relaxation techniques as methods of controlling arousal and anxiety, and improving sports performance. The learner has made reference to anxiety; to fulfil the criteria there should be an evaluation of how relaxation techniques can help to control or to reduce the impact of arousal on performance, as has been done for imagery. It would be interesting for the learner to provide examples of techniques he or she may have used to cope with arousal and anxiety and to also give examples of situations where he or she experienced too much or too little arousal and how this affected performance.

# Sample assignment brief: Learning aim A

| ASSIGNMENT TITLE | Personality and sports performance |
|---|---|
| LEARNING AIM | 2A |
| CRITERIA COVERED | 2A.P1, 2A.M1, 2A.D1 |
| ASSESSMENT EVIDENCE | Written report |

## Scenario

For part of your leadership award you have been volunteering as a sports psychologist for a semi-professional sports team. You have been asked to prepare a range of resources that could be used to help improve the team's performance. Your work will need to include information about how personality affects performance.

## Task I

**How personality affects sports performance.**

Produce information about what personality is and how it can increase or decrease sports performance. You will need to show how personality affects sports performance and analyse the different views of personality.

You might include sports examples to show how personality can directly affect performance.

This task should be presented as a written report.

# Learning aim B

| ASSIGNMENT TITLE | The influence of motivation and self-confidence on sports performance |
|---|---|
| LEARNING AIM | 2B |
| CRITERIA COVERED | 2B.P2, 2B.M2, 2B.D2, 2B.P3, 2B.P4, 2B.P5, 2B.M3 |
| ASSESSMENT EVIDENCE | Individual or small group PowerPoint presentations, written reports, leaflets or handbooks |

## Scenario

As a sports player you are always looking for ways to improve your performance. Being motivated and self-confident are important traits or characteristics needed by sports people at all levels. Your coach has asked you to produce some material to help improve your motivation and self-confidence. This material could be in the form of a leaflet or a handbook.

## Task 1

**Motivation and self-confidence and their effect on sports performance.**

Produce information about motivation and self-confidence. You will need to describe types and views of motivation and its benefits to sports performance and self-confidence.

You might include examples from experiences you have had in sport. What motivates you to perform? How does motivation affect you?

This task should be presented as a spider diagram which can be added to your information pack.

## Task 2

**Factors that influence self-efficacy in sport.**

Produce information about self-efficacy. You will need to describe self-efficacy and use sports examples to help you to show how it can influence sports performance. You might include examples from experiences you have had in sport. What factors have you noticed affect your self-efficacy?

This task should be presented as a table which can be added to your information pack.

## Task 3

### Goal setting and how these can influence sports performance and motivation.

Produce information about goal setting. You will need to describe different types of goals and how these can be set to help improve sports performance.

You might include examples from experiences you have had in sport: what types of goals have you used and how have these affected your performance?

This task should be presented as a written report which can be added to your information pack.

## Task 4

### The benefits of motivation and self-confidence on performance.

Produce information about self-confidence and motivation and analyse how these can benefit sports performance.

You might include examples from your own experiences in sport: when were you motivated and how did it affect your performance? What issues have you experienced with motivation and self-confidence?

This task should be presented as a written report which can be added to your information pack.

# Learning aim C

| ASSIGNMENT TITLE | Arousal and anxiety effects on sports performance |
|---|---|
| LEARNING AIM | 2C |
| CRITERIA COVERED | 2C.P6 |
| ASSESSMENT EVIDENCE | Individual or small group PowerPoint presentations, written reports, leaflets or handbooks. |

## Scenario

You have been asked to create an information pack by your sports coach to help you to improve your performance and that of your team mates. You have been studying anxiety and its effect on sports performance at school. Your coach has suggested that you use this information to make a PowerPoint presentation, to show your team mates how anxiety can affect performance and how to overcome any negative responses.

# Task 1

**Different types of anxiety.**

Produce information about the different types of anxiety. You will need to show how anxiety affects sports performance.

You might include sports examples to help you to describe the different views of anxiety and whether they have a negative or positive effect on performance. This task should be presented as a PowerPoint presentation; you can work as an individual or in groups of two or three.

# Task 2

**The effects of anxiety and arousal on sports performance and their control.**

Produce information about the four different theories of arousal and anxiety.

You might include diagrams which represent each theory and include sports examples to help explain how these views refer to sports performance.

This task should be presented as a written report which can be added to your information pack.

# Task 3

**How imagery and relaxation techniques can be used to control anxiety and arousal.**

Produce information about the different types of relaxation techniques.

You might include examples from your own sports experiences where you have either used, or seen other performers use, relaxation techniques to help control anxiety and arousal.

This task should be presented as a written report which can be added to your information pack.

# Knowledge recap answers

## Learning aim A: Topics A1–A3, p.5

1. The mixture of characteristics or traits which make every person unique.
2. When the coach knows the personality type of the athlete she can chose the correct psychological methods of training to help the athlete achieve his best.
3. The behaviours that a person usually responds with to the same situation.
4. A person's attitudes, values, interests and beliefs.
5. People who are usually inward looking, shy and happy with their own company.
6. People who are usually outgoing, loud and happy in other people's company.

## Learning aim A: Topics A4–A5, p.7

1. Questionnaires or observation.
2. Eysenck's personality inventory: a questionnaire used to measure personality types.
3. Trait behaviours are how a person responds consistently to a range of situations.
4. Situational behaviours are how a person responds to a particular environment.

## Learning aim B: Topics B1–B5, p.19

1. Motivation is what drives you to do something, it is the internal mechanisms and external stimuli that arouse and direct behaviour.
2. Intrinsic motivation comes from your own enjoyment, to take part in something you want to compete in for your own satisfaction.
3. Extrinsic motivation comes from rewards such as money, trophies and medals; you want to beat others and be the best.
4. These views are that personality traits determine a person's motivation.
5. These views are that the situation or environment affects a person's motivation.
6. These views are that trait and situation affect a person's motivation.
7. The effort someone will put into mastering or learning a new task, achieving excellence, overcoming obstacles and performing better than all others.
8. Motivation can make a performer chose a certain activity, it can make someone try harder to meet his goals and it can make someone try even if he is losing.

## Learning aim B: Topic B6, p.20

1. SMARTER goals are specific; measurable, achievable, realistic, time-related, exciting and recorded.

## Learning aim B: Topic B7–B9, p.21

1. A person's self-belief, the belief that he can perform the skills he wants to.
2. Self-confidence can help to improve performance and improve a person's concentration and effort.
3. Self-talk and imagery can increase self-confidence.

## Learning aim B: Topics B10–B11, p.23

1. Self-confidence in a specific situation.
2. Watching significant others performing successfully, demonstrating and modelling.
3. Teachers, coaches and peers.
4. Experiences where someone imagines his personal performance being successful.

## Learning aim B: Topics B12–B14, p.25

1. Outcome goals and performance goals.
2. Goal setting can help direct attention to certain aspects or skills in your performance. It can highlight weaknesses and help you to address them.
3. Goal setting can help to improve a performer's performance by maintaining his focus.

## Learning aim C, p.45

1. When he is in a situation of high pressure; this could be his first competition or the first time he performs a skill.
2. Trait anxiety is how our personality copes with different situations and state anxiety is temporary feelings of nervousness.
3. Somatic anxiety is how your body responds with physical reactions, for example, butterflies in your stomach and an increased heart rate. Cognitive anxiety might make you may feel worried and unable to concentrate.
4. Anxiety can decrease performance because the sports person is so worried about his ability and the situation that his performance suffers and he does not perform as well as he should.
5. The drive theory states that as arousal increases, performance also increases.
6. The optimum point is the level of arousal which makes a performer play at his best ability; any more arousal and his performance will decrease.
7. The physical effects of arousal, for example, increased heart and breathing rate.
8. Imagery and relaxation techniques.
9. Breathing techniques and progressive muscular relaxation.